Harold F. Tuggy

Temperance in the Christian Home

How to raise children in the discipline and admonition of the Lord

Translation of the Spanish Fifth Edition, 2024
Original title: Templanza en el Hogar Cristiano:
Cómo criar a los niños en disciplina y amonestación del Señor

Temperance in the Christian Home

How to Raise Children in the Discipline and Admonition of the Lord
by Harold F. Tuggy

Translated from Spanish to English by Sierra Translation Services.

ISBN: 979-8-23025-527-7 (Draft2Digital softcover)
ISBN: 979-8-30132-016-3 (Amazon softcover)
ASIN: B0DMV7S9DR (Amazon Kindle eBook)

Published by **Sunny Breeze Press** in 2024.

sunnybreezepress.com

A complete list of all the versions of Scripture cited and their respective copyright notices can be found in Appendix B.

Table of Contents

Foreword

My parents, Harold Tuggy and Dauphine Page, were married a little over a hundred years ago. During their married life, they had four sons and later two daughters. I was the fourth son.

Our parents showed us what "temperance in the Christian home" really is. Dad was pastor of many churches in eastern Venezuela. When a woman from the church asked for pastoral consultation, Dad always insisted that Mom be present. He did not preach to us about faithfulness. They lived before our eyes an exemplary life of faithfulness and temperance.

My three older brothers lived apart from our parents throughout their teenage years for educational reasons. I well remember that every Sunday mid-afternoon, Dad would take out his little table and typewriter to write a letter to each of my brothers at their boarding school. My three brothers, Edward, Alfred, and Harold, later returned to Venezuela united in the work of the Lord Jesus. I was a Bible translator all my life in Peru. Both of my sisters were faithful wives in their homes. What exemplary parents!

Eventually, Dad wrote the vibrant and important book entitled "Temperance in the Christian Home". It is a tremendous honor for me to present to you this very important book relevant to contemporary needs.

John Tuggy

Introduction

"...The grace of God has appeared ... It teaches us to reject godless ways and worldly desires, and in the present age to lead lives that are temperate, just, and godly." (Titus 2:11–12 NCB)

The Roman Empire was at the height of its glory. The wealthy lived in luxury and lust, and the downtrodden appeased their misery with degrading vices. Carnal excesses of all kinds characterized that time.

At such a time the apostle Paul wrote the above words. At such a time the voice of the message of God's grace sounded, announcing salvation and forgiveness of sin and, as a fruit of this salvation, the life of temperance. The Lord Himself had said that when the Holy Spirit came, He *would "convict the world of sin, and of righteousness and of judgment." (John 16:8)* And later, Governor Felix was appalled when the apostle Paul reasoned with him about *"righteousness, self-control, and the judgment to come." (Acts 24:25)*

The Christian teaching in relation to practical living is temperance, self-control, a sound mind, moderation, purity, sobriety, modesty and virtue. Our times are characterized by the same things as those times. But biblical teaching must produce a Christian people distinguished by their wholesome habits in the midst of a corrupt world.

Now, the home is the oldest of human institutions, the foundation of social groups. It is founded on the most sacred of human relationships: marriage. At home, children learn the lessons that will shape their character.

Robert Burns, the Scottish poet (1759–1796), in his immortal *The Cotter's Saturday Night,* described a Christian home in Scotland and their family prayer:

> The cheerfu' supper done, wi' serious face,
> They, round the ingle, form a circle wide.
> The sire turns o'er, with patriarchal grace, the big ha'bible.
> And "Let us worship God!" he says with solemn air.
>
> They chant their artless notes in simple guise,
> They tune their hearts, by far the noblest aim.
>
> The priest-like father reads the sacred page...
>
> Perhaps the Christian volume is the theme,
> How guiltless blood for guilty man was shed...
>
> Then, kneeling down to Heaven's Eternal King,
> The saint, the father, and the husband prays:
> Hope "springs exulting on triumphant wing,"
> That thus they all shall meet in future days,
> There, ever bask in uncreated rays,
> No more to sigh, or shed the bitter tear,
> Together hymning their Creator's praise...
>
> Compar'd with this, how poor Religion's pride,
> The Power, incens'd, the pageant will desert,

But haply, in some cottage far apart,
May hear, well-pleas'd, the language of the soul;
And in His Book of Life the inmates poor enroll.[1]

He concludes that, from scenes like this, the greatness of Scotland is born, which makes it beloved at home and revered abroad.

In this scene, the villager's house is a humble hut, but the home is of a noble spirit. Just as the life of man is more than the body and does not consist in the abundance of the things he possesses; the home is more than the house where the family dwells.

However, the home can be likened to a house, in that it has foundations, doors, walls, roof, windows and gardens to beautify and bear fruit. Well says the psalmist: *"Unless the Lord builds the house, they labor in vain who build it" (Psalm 127:1)*. But, when we build with Him, our home will be characterized by true temperance. Let us look at the plans He has drawn up.

---

1   The unabridged excerpt is included in Appendix A.

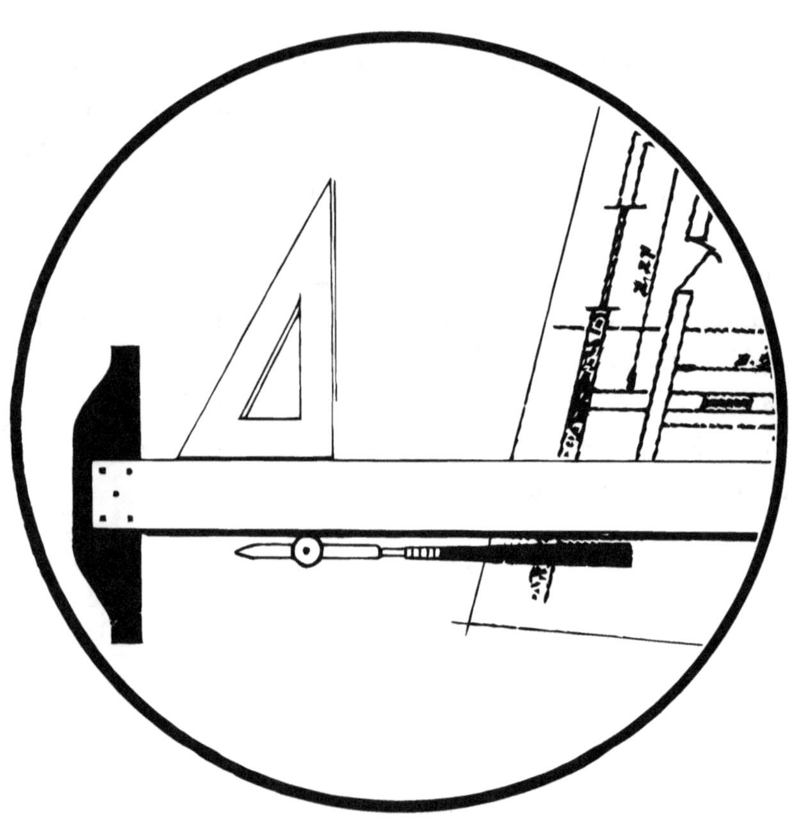

CHAPTER I

The Foundations of the Christian Home

TEMPERANCE IN THE FOUNDATION

The foundation of a Christian home requires temperance. Marriage is a serious step and should not be entered into inconsiderately. Our young people need Christian guidance so that they can establish homes on truly Christian foundations.

True love is something more than "a certain itch in the heart region that can't be scratched". Marriage formed on the basis of such a fleeting love fails. Marriage is more than sexual attraction. And the marriage bond is for life. Marriage has been defined as the creative union of two people. "Male and female he created them." It is not just the physical union of two bodies. It is the union of whole people: their affections, their intellects, their ideas and their ideals. Nor is it the submission of one personality to another. It is the union of two personalities in which each

1

retains its individuality and at the same time the two form a new harmonious entity.

It is a *creative union*. Marriage that does not have a creative purpose is not marriage, but a license for the use of sex or a convenience to have a place to eat and sleep.

The first thing that is created is the home. It is normal for children to be born. The happiness of the home is not complete without them. *"...children are a heritage from the Lord; the fruit of the womb is a reward." (Psalm 127:3)* And it is in the home that the characters of these children will be formed and developed. Therefore, parents must creatively direct their child's physical, intellectual, emotional, moral and spiritual development.

In addition, some couples unite their creative powers for other purposes.

Robert Browning and his wife Elizabeth Barrett Browning, both poets, combined their creative literary powers to make a most remarkable contribution to nineteenth-century English literature. Mr. and Mrs. Pierre Curie, both French chemists, collaborated in scientific research that resulted in the discovery of the element radium in the early twentieth century. We all know physicians whose wives have medical or nursing degrees and work in their profession. There are pastors whose wives participate in their pastoral work, professors whose wives collaborate in teaching, thus doing creative work in their respective fields.

To achieve such a happy and productive union requires a love based on friendliness and compatibility of ideas and ideals, on mutual trust, respect and consideration, on mutual give and take, and on unreserved contribution to the creative enterprise.

Therefore, we recommend certain rules to help Christian youth to choose their life partner, their "suitable helper".

1. **THEY MUST BOTH BE CHRISTIANS.**
    "Do not be unequally yoked together with unbelievers..." (*2 Corinthians 6:14*) A Christian may feel some attraction to an unbelieving person, there may be sympathy and compatibility of ideas, and this may result in some feeling called love. But can there be sympathy and compatibility of ideals? *"...what partnership has righteousness with unrighteousness? And what fellowship has light with darkness? ... For you are the temple of the living God." (2 Corinthians 6:14, 16 RGT)*

2. **THERE SHOULD BE APPROXIMATE EQUALITY OF INTELLIGENCE, EDUCATION AND SOCIAL CAPACITY.**
    The unequal yoke with unbelievers is forbidden. There may also be an unequal yoke that is not suitable among Christians.

A Christian presented his complaints to the pastor against a young lady, a member of the same church, because she lacked Christian love, since she had rejected the marriage proposal he had made to her. He was an uneducated man, she a schoolteacher; he was crippled and unable to work, she was in full health. It is obvious that such a union would be an unequal and painful yoke. The pastor had to explain to the poor brother that Christian love is one thing, and married love is quite another. Christian love knows no boundaries. Marital love has boundaries that cannot be crossed without bad results for the spouses, and sometimes worse results for the children.

A young lady raised in an environment of culture and education should not marry a crude man, even if he is a Christian. His lack of delicacy will irritate her. He will believe that her desire to order the home and her life according to the best social customs is presumptuousness. In the end the yoke becomes almost unbearable. A yoke is used to join two animals together to perform some useful work. If the yoke is comfortable, they work well; if the yoke is uncomfortable and unequal, it becomes a cross.

3. **THEY MUST HAVE COMMON INTERESTS AND COMPATIBLE VOCATIONS.**

If you both have some ability and taste in music, you will spend many happy hours together, playing or singing or listening to musical pieces. Music will be a basis for you to get closer and grow in love. The same is true if the two pursue certain kinds of reading or study together. But if his hobby is some scientific study, while hers is music, it may turn out that the beautiful melody she plays is an annoying noise for him when he is concentrating on his study. And at the table he will want to talk about some wonderful discovery that for her will be annoying. This can lead to a separation of interests and a cooling of love.

As for vocation, some Christians are called by God to a special work, and it is necessary for them to choose a wife who has such a calling. We should note here that, for the woman, the vocation of forming a Christian home is the highest of all, and is compatible with almost any vocation that the Christian husband may have, provided that she is willing to form the home with the limited resources that may come from the husband's work.

4. THEY MUST HAVE TRUSTWORTHY CHARACTERS.

Even among so-called Christians there are some of inconsistent character. Such are not good candidates for marriage. What confidence can one have in a man who today enthusiastically starts an enterprise and tomorrow abandons it? Can a man have confidence in a wife who wastes money? The person who conceals the truth, or who tells strangers the intimate and internal things of the home, destroys the mutual trust that should exist between spouses and alienates love.

5. THE TWO NATURES MUST BE COMPLEMENTARY.

It is a well-known fact that two people of too similar natures do not bond well. Their natures must be such that one completes what is lacking in the other. The Creator made it that way. The feminine mind is somewhat different from the masculine, so that each finds in the other its complement. In addition, a cheerful and expansive person bonds better with one who is calm, as long as neither is excessively so.

6. THEY MUST HAVE THE ABILITY TO "GIVE AND TAKE".

In every marriage, there is the need for each to adjust to the other. Neither of you should have the idea that you are going to reform the other or remake the other's personality to your own liking. Each influences the other and over time the two personalities mold, so that two new and harmonious personalities are formed. This process requires a mutual willingness to give and receive without taking offense, to concede a point to the other, to give preference to the other with love and consideration, to carry the other's burden and to bear the other with love.

It also requires a willingness to contribute unreservedly and without restraint to the joint venture. If each has the idea of giving half and nothing more, they will fight over what half is. If one thinks that he or she gives more than the other, jealousy and envy enter, and love flies out the window.

There are fathers who are unable to get up at night to help care for a sick child. They think: "I have to work all day, I earn the money, I support the household". They don't think that the wife also works all day long doing housework and washing the child's diapers, and that she also is tired. Note how many times the "I" is repeated in his thought.

Here is a simple lesson in human relations:

- The five most important words:
I am proud of you.

- The four most important words:
What is your opinion?

- The three most important words:
If you please.

- The two most important words:
Thank you.

The word of least importance: *I*.

And among human relationships, marriage is the foremost.

7. **HEALTH MUST BE TAKEN INTO ACCOUNT.**
In addition to spiritual, moral, intellectual, emotional and social considerations, physical considerations should not be overlooked. A young lady, before marrying a sick and disabled man, should think about who will support the household and head it with dignity. Similarly, forming a creative union with a sickly woman will be somewhat more difficult. If children are born, it will be with great difficulty, and they are likely to inherit weaknesses and illness tendencies from the mother. The wife's physical weaknesses will make it very difficult for her to participate in any of the husband's other creative work.

8. **THE MARRIAGE SHOULD BE POSTPONED IF ONE OF THE PARTIES IS GOING TO STUDY.**
People who do not aspire to acquire advanced education, or who do not have the vocation that such education requires, may marry very young. But vocations to Christian ministry and professional vocations require more academic training. This makes it necessary to postpone the marriage. It is part of the price to be paid by those who aspire to better things in life and in Christian service; and even in secular vocations and professions. It's worth it. Excellent things are costly.

As evangelical Christian people advance, there will be a smaller number of their young people who marry at sixteen; and there will be a larger number who wait until twenty-five. These will be the happiest and most useful.

All of the above requires self-control and Christian temperance. Others may fall madly in love. The young Christian cannot. As marriage is the most important step in life for the young Christian, he should seek God's direction in prayer; he should follow the sound counsels of His Word; he should think rightly and master the affections of the heart, so that they may be subject to the dictates of a sound mind. This is temperance in the first step, that of founding a Christian home on a firm foundation, on the Rock.

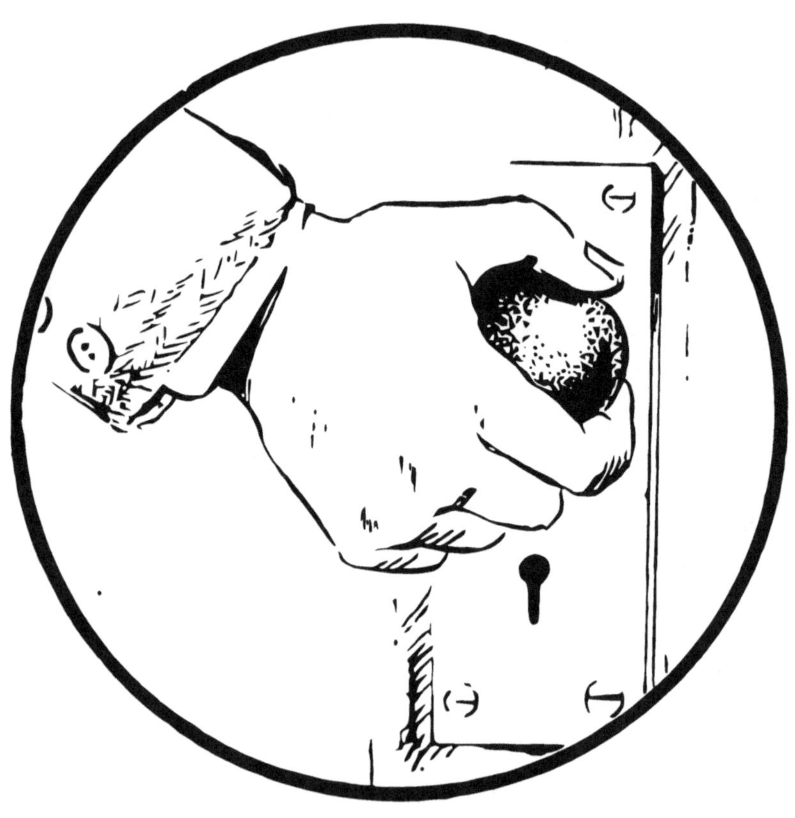

"(You shall call) your gates praise."

(ISAIAH 60:18)

CHAPTER II

The Doors and Their Keys

TEMPERANCE IN THE MANAGEMENT OF THE CHRISTIAN HOME

"Therefore do not be unwise, but understand what the will of the Lord is." "Finally, my brethren, be strong in the Lord and in the power of his might." (Ephesians 5:17 and 6:10)

With the first of these verses begins, and with the last one ends a passage in which the apostle Paul speaks of the relationships between people who form the household. In the former, the need for prudence and to know the will of the Lord is noted, and in the latter, the need to strive in the Lord to put into practice the teachings received. There are three words here that speak of strength: gather *strength* (original of *be strong*) in the *power* of his *might*.

For the good management of a Christian home, founded on a Christian foundation, one must have prudence, one must know the will of the Lord, and one must use strength of character, temperance itself.

Now, in a house there are doors that lead to all the rooms. These doors have their keys that allow going into the innermost places. Thus we can compare the management of the Christian home with these keys that open the way to success, to praise itself. The teaching of the quoted portion of Ephesians implies the following practices as keys:

1. **FAMILY PRAYER.**
    This is the first key to success in the Christian home. When there is spiritual difficulty in a family, it is almost certain that there is also neglect of family prayer. The family that prays together stays together.

Young Christians should establish family prayer in their homes, on the same day that the home is formed. How precious it is when, even during courtship, they are accustomed to reading the Scriptures and praying together! Thus they seek the Lord's guidance regarding their marriage. When this is done, the foundations are already laid for family prayer. The altar has already been erected.

Brother, if this blessed custom has not been established in your home, start today. It may be that after all this time you are a little embarrassed to begin it. It doesn't matter. Let's get to work! Start today!

A father of a family promised the Lord to begin family prayer after years of marriage and with his family already formed. As the hour approached, he left his house, out of nervousness, and walked around the block several times chewing on a toothpick. But he soon mastered his feelings and went into the house, called all the children and the wife, and they held their first family service. If you are in the same situation, go and do the same. The point is to get started.

A church was located in a bad neighborhood of a city. The pastor struggled hard, but only managed to get very few to attend services. He then put into practice the work plan of visiting all the homes in the neighborhood and teaching the families to observe family prayer. After a few years of work, the bad character of the neighborhood was completely changed and the church was filled with Christians. The power of family prayer is immense.

That is why it seems that the devil hates family worship in a special way. And he is very ingenious at inventing interruptions. If it's not an unwelcome visit, it's a phone call, or a sick child crying, or a cat getting into the kitchen and spilling milk on the table. You have to overcome these things. A time should be chosen when the whole family can be present and when there are normally no interruptions. Then, don't allow anything to enter and take away the sanctity of this hour. This requires temperance. In time the custom will become so established that none of the family will think of anything else when that sacred hour arrives. It will come to be a matter of household routine and a blessed inspiration.

But there is another danger: It must be part of the established routine, but never become a merely routine thing. It is easy to repeat the same prayer every day, without thinking about what is being said, and to read the Bible in a monotonous voice, without the reader or the listeners noticing what is being read. This natural tendency must be combated. It is necessary to study how to make family worship a lively and interesting activity. The program can be varied somewhat, sometimes using songs or brief explanations of the passage read. Some portion of the Scriptures can be learned and repeated by heart. You can mention some things you wish to thank God for, or make some requests, before praying. Above all, the work of the Holy Spirit, who teaches us to worship in spirit and in truth, is needed. It is the same Spirit that instills temperance to carry out this purpose.

2. **UNITED PARTICIPATION IN ACTIVITIES.**

    This is the second key. A young married couple will enjoy it very much if they plan together the things they can do to beautify their home, and then do them together. Paint the furniture, renovate a broken door and paint it, put some simple and tasteful decorations in the living room, plant some bushes in the yard. There are so many things that can be done to turn a house into a home. And as they do them together, they will find that companionship has grown between them and that the love of courtship is becoming a deep and mature love.

Eating at the table is very important. There are families in which the wife puts food on the table for her husband, for the older children and for a visitor; but she eats in the kitchen, with a plate in her hand, and the little ones eat sitting on the kitchen floor. Some would say that poverty forces them to do so. It is not a matter of poverty. The poorest of the poor can gather around a common table, give thanks to God and eat together.

More than just stew and fried plantains are served at the table. Love is served. The family talk and fellowship among family members is as important as the food. Mealtime should be a sacred time when everyone comes together because they are united in spirit. They belong to an entity, to a family, and it is here that the ties that solidify the family are strengthened.

In addition to striving together to beautify the home and gather around the family table, there are a multitude of things they can do together: walking, reading, singing, studying, playing, working, attending church services. O beloved! All your lives you should be together. Then in the hours when, by the duties of work or business you have to be separated, you will remain united in spirit; and when the hour of the husband's return home draws near, the wife's heart will sing: "Behold, my beloved is coming...", and his steps will become light with the thought, "How beautiful you are, my darling!"

3. **THE CULTIVATION OF LOVE.**
   It is a key that logically follows the previous one. Love is like a beautiful flower: It can be cultivated and it becomes even more beautiful; or, if neglected, it withers and dries up.

Some young men shave and dress neatly to visit their girlfriend. But after marriage they let days go by without shaving or bathing. They are already married, they already have a wife. Why go to so much trouble to make yourself attractive? Similarly, some married women spend all day at home without combing their hair, with their hair rolled up in curlers. What a disappointment some men will suffer when they find themselves married to such a careless woman! What a disappointment for some women to have to live with a man who does not have self-esteem, nor show a little consideration for her through a little personal grooming!

The cultivation of love consists of small things. The wife who gets up early, combs her hair and dresses herself neatly and prepares breakfast with pleasure, has given an encouraging start to her husband's working day. And he will have the hope of returning from work to a clean house and a neat, beautiful, smiling and kind wife. Likewise, he should show her the same consideration.

Man: it's been a while since you kissed your wife! Tonight, when she is in the kitchen preparing your dinner, take her in your arms and give her a kiss and tell her: I love you, I love you. (Be careful that she doesn't let dinner burn or hit you in the face because of the surprise you cause her). Perhaps the flower of her youth is withering for lack of a little bit of affection that only you can give her.

In conversation and in dealing with her, stop nagging and treat her with love and tenderness. Some men are very gentlemanly and polite in their dealings with friends and with all those with whom they come in contact in business; but at home they are wild beasts. This should not be the case.

"Husbands, love your wives" (Ephesians 5:25) is God's commandment. In the marriage vows the husband promises to "love her, comfort her, honor her, and keep her in times of sickness or health, and, renouncing all others," to keep himself for her alone as long as they both shall live. As long as she is young and in good health, it is natural and easy to love her. But as the years go by, some of her teeth fall out, her face wrinkles and she no longer

enjoys that exuberant health. What then? Many men then start looking at younger women. Brother: she has given you the years of her youth. Remember the Lord's commandment: *"Husbands, love your wives"*. Then remember your wedding vows: "To love her ... in time of sickness or in health, and, forsaking all others...." Temper your thoughts, renounce in your mind all others, give her again the tenderness of your love, the patient bearing of her weakness... *"giving honor to the wife, as to the weaker vessel"*. (1 Peter 3:7)

If during the first years of married life you have been attentive to each other in cultivating love, when the advanced years come, the love between the two of you will be as sweet as ripe fruit. Apply your energy to cultivate it.

4. **GIVE CAREFUL ATTENTION TO CONVERSATIONS, READING MATERIALS, AND ENTERTAINMENT.**
   This is the fourth key. *"Of making many books there is no end,"* (Ecclesiastes 12:12) wrote Solomon centuries before the invention of the printing press. Nowadays there is a veritable torrent of magazines, news bulletins, comic strips and books of all kinds. In addition, there are numerous radio and television programs, many of which have a bad influence. In our Christian homes we have to exercise much temperance, to check what is read and what is heard; otherwise, this sweeping current will lead us and our children into the abyss of complete confusion.

There are Christians who do not go to the movies because it is a worldly thing, and because certain movies show scenes of crimes or things that have immoral implications. But they look at the comic strips, with their series of thieves, muggers and illicit love affairs, and allow their children to read them. And, those same movies that they consider bad, and that they don't go to see in the theater, they watch on television at home. They don't let their children go to the movies to see *The Loves of Jezebel*, but they let them read the novel *Juliana of the Black Hand*. And the conversations around the table? Are they about the school baseball game, about an article of interest that appeared in *Reader's Digest* or a Christian magazine? Or are they about the man from the neighboring town who killed his wife, or some other scandalous affair, with all the details? These latter topics are not healthy food for our minds, nor for our children's.

The solution to this problem does not lie in denial. It is not enough to forbid children to read certain things. We must guide them with our example as parents, and then help them to select the right material. At the table, conversation should be carefully directed to topics of mental, intellectual and spiritual benefit. If someone introduces an ill-advised topic (such as the latest neighborhood scandal), you can talk about something else, thus diverting the conversation.

As for reading, the stories of some of the early missionaries who went to savage peoples are as interesting and exciting as any novel, and are infinitely more edifying. Our taste and that of our children can be educated to appreciate the best. Once good taste has been acquired, things in bad taste are unpleasant. The same is true about radio and music programs. Once the taste for classical music has been educated, jukebox and canteen music is very unpleasant. We must learn to choose. It is like the one who eats fish: He has to learn to eat the meat and throw away the bones.

The Scriptures teach the same truth. *"Finally, brethren, whatever things are true, whatever things are noble, whatever things are just, whatever things are pure, whatever things are lovely, whatever things are of good report, if there is any virtue and if there is anything praiseworthy—meditate on these things." (Philippians 4:8)* We can elaborate: Talk about these things, read about these things, hear about and watch these things on television. Let us temper our thinking and our conversations and watch for these things in our homes.

5. **DEALING WITH STRANGERS IN THE HOME.**
   This is a key that deserves attention. It is a fatal mistake for a young married couple to live in his or her parents' home. In-laws tend to meddle in the affairs of young people. Equally fatal is for one of the in-laws to live in the young person's home. If the young man has the responsibility to support his mother, he should support her in her home, or get a small house nearby where he can keep and care for her, but not in his own home. Such a situation is as difficult for the old woman as it is for the young couple. If you are a person of compatible ideals and you are a good match, the relationship can be a happy one. Otherwise it becomes unbearable. Even if the relationship is happy, there is danger: the danger that such a person may become too familiar and intimate. In some cases this has resulted in illicit love with one spouse, and has brought complete failure in the home. To maintain family unity without excluding hospitality, discretion and temperance are needed.

6.   THE USE OF TIME.

The use of time for good ends is a key that requires Christian temperance. Solomon says: *"To everything there is a season, A time for every purpose under heaven. ... He has made everything beautiful in its time." (Ecclesiastes 3:1, 11)*

When arranging life at home, a time is designated for family worship: This time must be respected. Certain meal times are set: All family members should respect these times and arrive at the table on time. Some time should be set aside for recreation, some evening during the week for family games, or some time after work for sports. All members must participate. Recreation is necessary, but it should not take up too much time. In the evenings it is very helpful to spend some time reading or studying. Some have achieved excellent instruction, judiciously employing their free time in study. Others waste these hours at the movies or listening to nonsense on the radio.

I visited a Christian school that was largely supported by donations from Mr. Henry Ford (manufacturer of Ford automobiles). The friend who accompanied me on the visit told me how Mr. Ford visited the school and sometimes spent several days there. He would get up early and go to the dumpster to see what things were being thrown away. He was interested to know that they were not throwing away anything useful. One of the richest people in the world searching a dumpster! For one of the secrets of his wealth was the way he made use of the waste from his factory.

The greatest waste in the world is time. Mr. Ford knew this too, and therein lay another secret of his success. Let's record the time wasted in our homes. We will find great spiritual and intellectual richness.

In the Decalogue, God gave us the first and most important lesson in the use of time. "Six days you shall labor and do all your work, but the seventh day is the Sabbath of the Lord your God." Let us observe the elements of this lesson: Designate a time for one thing and another time for another, and respect and attend to that designation. In the home where the members have learned to respect the Lord's day and not use that day for work or sports games, but for rest and worship of God, they will also know how to respect the time designated for work and study or for another activity. The twenty-four hours of the day will be put to good use through temperance.

7. **THE USE OF MONEY.**
    This is another key that brings a similar elementary lesson, for God said, *"Bring all the tithes into the storehouse...";* and: *"On the first day of the week let each one of you lay something aside, storing up as he may prosper...." (Malachi 3:10, 1 Corinthians 16:2)* We do not ignore the argument that we are not under the law, and therefore we have no obligation to tithe; but it is an irrefutable fact that God blesses those who do. The lesson this teaches us has the following elements: to designate a portion of our money or other assets for one purpose, and to respect that designation and not use it for another purpose. *"It is a snare for a man to devour that which is holy...." "If you make a promise to God, don't be slow to keep it. ... It is better not to promise anything than to promise something and not do it." (Proverbs 20:25 KJ21 and Ecclesiastes 5:4, 5 NCV)*

Once the elementary lesson is learned, it is easy to transfer it and apply it to other purposes: Set aside a portion for rents, another portion for savings, and so on. It doesn't matter if the portions are small, the important thing is to set them aside and respect them. Let us remember that "large capitals are made from small economies"; and, even more important, that *He who is faithful in what is least is faithful also in much."* Those who faithfully temper their needs to the extent of their possessions will know how to keep their household in order.

The one responsible for initiating and maintaining order in the management of the household is the man, the father of the family. He is the one who directs both materially and spiritually. *"Wives, submit to your own husbands, as to the Lord. For the husband is head of the wife, as also Christ is head of the church...." (Ephesians 5:22–23)* The one who carries the key ring is the father of the family, and the family follows through the doors he opens for them.

The keys he holds in his hands are seven: family prayer, united participation in activities, the cultivation of love, careful attention to conversations, readings and entertainment, the proper treatment of strangers in the home, the good use of time and the proper use of money. They are the keys that will open the doors to great spiritual blessings, to a beautiful testimony; and, in addition, to material prosperity. They will open the gates that you will call Praise. And the home will be a Bethany where Christ desires to dwell.

CHAPTER III

The Four Walls

TEMPERANCE IN THE DISCIPLINE OF THE CHRISTIAN HOME

There are four issues of discipline in the home, of such importance that we will call them *the four walls*. Just as four walls are essential to form a house, so these four disciplines are essential in the Christian home. Just as the walls enclose the house and make it a unit, protecting the inhabitants, so these disciplines unify the home and protect the family from many deadly temptations: They enclose the proper and exclude the improper.

With strict Christian temperance parents must practice these disciplines in their own lives. With prayer and diligence they are to teach them to their children. For if they do not live by them, they will try in vain to instill them in their children.

We will have strong walls of Salvation and we will not build in vain if we build these four walls around our homes. They are entirely biblical, and Jehovah will build with us.

1. **REVERENCE**

is the front wall. *"You shall not take the name of the Lord your God in vain...."* [1] *"Watch your step when you go to the house of God ... because God is in heaven and you are on earth, so let your words be few."* [2] *"But the Lord is in His holy temple. Let all the earth keep silence before Him...."* [3] *"O Lord, I have heard Your speech and was afraid...."* [4]

The lack of reverence characterizes our times. Even in some evangelical temples, reverence is notable by its absence. The children walk back and forth during the service, the elders converse during the sermon, and when the service is dismissed, the conversations leave the impression of people leaving a movie theater rather than a worship service. It is evidence that reverence is not practiced or taught to children in their homes. *"Guard your steps when you go to the house of God ... let your words be few."*

The home is the place where the child should learn reverence. The Father opens the Bible and everyone listens attentively and reverently to his reading. It is the voice of God speaking to us. Then all kneel before his presence and present a prayer before the Almighty. Even the smallest child feels the divine presence and learns to be silent.

I once pinched my brother and laughed with him during family prayer. Father sent me to my room. At the end of the prayer he also went to the room. I saw tears in his eyes and understood how deeply he felt my lack of reverence. After speaking to me and explaining

---

1   Exodus 20:7
2   Ecclesiastes 5:1, 2 EHV
3   Habakkuk 2:20
4   Habakkuk 3:2

the seriousness of the offense, he gave me a few lashes that forever took away my desire to pinch my brother during prayer or commit any other act of irreverence.

2. **RESPECT FOR PARENTS AND ELDERS**
    is the wall on one side, which forms a corner with the first wall. As two walls meet at the corner and by means of the joint support each other, so these two joined disciplines support each other. Where one is lacking, the other will be lacking also.

"There is a generation that curses its father, and does not bless its mother. There is a generation that is pure in its own eyes, yet is not washed from its filthiness. There is a generation—oh, how lofty are their eyes! And their eyelids are lifted up. There is a generation whose teeth are like swords and whose fangs are like knives...." *(Proverbs 30:11–14)*

"Honor your father and your mother",[5] is the first commandment with promise. We should note that in the law of Moses, the persistent infraction of this commandment carried a death penalty.

This is another lesson learned that I thank my parents for. Dad was not a harsh man but rather quiet and gentle, while at the same time very fair in his treatment. When he said something, we children understood that he meant it. If he told us to do something, he might have the patience to say it the second time. But we knew it was best not to wait for him to have to speak the third time! And we never dared to tell him: Just a minute.

---

5   Exodus 20:12

When we were newlyweds, a Christian family lived next door. We attended the same church and our houses had a common garage. The neighboring family had an adopted boy about eight years old. One day he was with his adoptive mother in the garage. She asked him to pass her a small bundle; the boy, insolently, replied no. For me that was a terrible and unbearable attitude. I interjected, saying:

"Boy, that's no way to talk to your mother!"

I had learned from my parents, that a child doesn't talk back like that. Both mother and child were stunned.

A few years ago, one of my sons returned from his vacation in the United States. He told us that for some months he had been a neighbor of a Christian family who remembered us; and that they had an adopted son, now a man, who caused them great sadness, for he was a drunkard and disorderly. It was that same family. *"There is a generation that curses its father … Yet is not washed from its filthiness."* No, even if he attended a thousand churches and learned half the Bible by heart as a child, he would not yet have cleansed himself of his filth.

In the years we have been teaching in a Bible Institute we have seen many students come and go. One thing we have observed: When someone arrives from a home where this lesson has not been taught, it doesn't take long to discover it. He is spoiled, ill-mannered, sassy, proud, even insolent. If in one or two years in the Institute, the young man does not correct this defect with the grace of God, he will never serve as a worker of the Lord. No matter how much consecration he professes, he is useless; he has not been cleansed of his filthiness.

3. TRUTHFULNESS

is the third wall. *"Do not lie to one another, since you have put off the old man with his deeds." (Colossians 3:9)* This is the clear commandment to stop lying.

It is unfortunate that sometimes Christians themselves are found to be untruthful. The verse teaches us that lying is of the old nature. Deception is innate in the human heart, so much so that a child knows how to deceive without being taught to do so. The death of the old man and the newness of life in Christ is the only remedy.

Now, at first glance, truthfulness is the quality of telling things as they are, not lying. This concept includes:

- honesty or probity
- integrity or selflessness
- loyalty or fidelity and
- sincerity or frankness.

Opposed to these virtues are:

- deception, i.e., lying
- selfishness, that is to say, greed
- infidelity and betrayal and
- hypocrisy and dissimulation.

Each of these four virtues can be analyzed to see the blessing it brings; equally one could see the curse that its opposite brings.

With a little meditation we see their necessity in the very daily management of the household, in the loving service rendered to each other by the members of the family so that there may be peace and not quarrels, in the relationship between spouses and between parents and children, and in reverence for God so that it does not turn out that *"These people honor me with their lips, but their hearts are far from me."*[6]

When it comes to children, parents must distinguish between lying and imagination or fantasy. It is a sign of intelligence that the child exercises his imagination. But both he and those who hear his stories should understand that such things are not true.

When he was four years old, Eduardito took part in a dinner party where he was served a turkey, which had been taken care of for several weeks so it would fatten up. The next day he stated:

"Mommy, I went to see the chickens and said to them: 'What happened to the turkey?'

And they told me:

'Poor little turkey, she died.'"

We laughed together at the story, and we didn't tell him: That's a lie! On the other hand, when he would say offhand that his two-year-old sister had hit him first, we would investigate the case.

A fairly serious issue in the family is that of denying guilt. This produces guilt complexes that can affect the child throughout his

---

6   Matthew 15:8

or her life. Proverbs 28:13 promises: *"The one who conceals his sins will not prosper, but whoever confesses and renounces them will find mercy."* (HCSB)

We recommend the study of the following biblical quotations for the family to erect the wall of truthfulness: Psalm 15:1–4; 7:9; 139:23, 24; Proverbs 26:28.

"Examine me, O Lord, and test me; try my mind and my heart. For Your lovingkindness is before my eyes, And I have walked in Your truth." (Psalm 26:2–3) *"Behold, You desire truth in the inward parts."* (Psalm 51:6).

4. **PURITY**

    is the fourth wall. It is between truthfulness and reverence: Sincerity and fear of God support this wall.

"So put to death whatever is worldly in you: sexual immorality, uncleanness, lust, evil desire, and greed, which is idolatry. It is because of these things that the wrath of God is coming on the sons of disobedience. You too once walked in these things, when you were living in them. But now, you too are to rid yourselves of all of these: wrath, anger, malice, slander, and filthy language from your mouth." (Colossians 3:5–8 EHV)

Moral filthiness is another part of our old nature. We should not even talk about such things. Dirty stories, obscene words, indecent pictures have no place in the Christian home. There are magazines that present the female body almost naked and in an exaggerated way. So many publications glorify lust and are full of immoral implications.

Parents, better to allow the family's food to be poisoned than to allow such things into the house! Are there under the mattress of the son's bed, the daughter's bed, hidden things that they are furtively reading?

My brother and I were doing some work around the house. Dad was in the living room, reading. We started repeating an insolence we had heard in the street and laughing about it. From the living room came Dad's voice:

"Harold, Arthur, what are you laughing about?"

"Nothing."

"Well, why are you laughing at nothing?"

Dad was not one of those naive or careless fathers who accepts an evasive answer. He kept asking questions until we confessed the whole truth. Then he gave us another one of those leather lessons that are not easily forgotten.

The world is corrupt, Satan is clever, many deadly dangers surround our families. With God's help let us build these four walls solidly, for the moral and spiritual protection of our families, which we will call Salvation: reverence, respect for parents and elders, truthfulness, and purity.

CHAPTER IV

The Roof

TEMPERANCE IN THE NEGATIVE ASPECT OF CHILD DISCIPLINE

There are two aspects of discipline, positive and negative. Both are as necessary as the positive and negative poles of an electrical circuit.

Let us first consider the negative aspect. Negative discipline is that which says *no,* which imposes prohibitions, which prescribes punishments and executes them. It is like the roof above the walls. These make a wall of salvation for the family. The roof shelters and covers from storms and tempests. Thus, prohibitions and corrections protect from the evils that may come upon the family.

Twice in Scripture the apostle Paul admonishes parents not to provoke their children to anger: Ephesians 6:4 and Colossians 3:21. This indicates that he had observed the abuse of negative discipline, a very common thing even among evangelical people.

35

A very noticeable defect in those who are learning to drive an automobile is that they move the steering wheel too far. If the car goes to the left, they move the steering wheel to the right, but too much. The result is that the car goes to the right and then they have to move it to the left. Thus, the car zigzags and is in danger of falling off on one side of the road or the other.

So it is in the discipline of our children. We are alternately too soft and too harsh with them, with the result that the child never learns to walk straight.

Having spent my apprenticeship with my Christian parents, and then in the forge of raising six children of our own, on the anvil of observation and with the hammer of experience, we have worked out some rules that will be of help to others. These are the eight beams that support the roof.

1. **PARENTS MUST BE UNITED.**
    In all matters of discipline and household rules, spouses should be in agreement. This is an essential requirement. If there is a difference of opinion between them, they should settle it privately and not in front of the children. *They should always present a united front to their children.*

If the mother punishes a child, and his father picks him up to console him with *"Oh, my poor child, your mother is so bad,"* all the value of the punishment is lost. If the father denies a permission to a child and then the mother grants it, a conflict forms between the parents and confusion in the child's mind. He has no basis for forming his idea of what is good or bad. But the child will learn that one parent grants his or her desire, even against the other, and will take advantage of this weakness of authority.

Sometimes a third party in the home, such as a grandmother or a servant, interferes with the punishment in the manner already mentioned. In such a case, parents have the duty to tell the third party, politely but firmly, that this matter does not concern them and that they should stay out of it.

In the discipline of children, let your yes be yes, and your no, no; and let the father and mother always say the same thing.

2. **LIES MUST BE VIGOROUSLY ATTACKED AND YOU MUST NOT TELL LIES.**
"The heart is deceitful above all things, and desperately wicked...",[1] says God by the mouth of Jeremiah. This is the nature that we all inherit and pass on by inheritance to our children, which manifests itself in them from birth. The child does not have to learn to tell lies, he already knows how.

Now, lying is not only what is *said* with the intent to deceive; it is anything that is *done* to deceive. Many parents allow their children to deceive them. They close their eyes to the smallest hints of deception. This allows the child to become proficient in the art of lying.

We were three siblings, eight, six and four years old. On the second corner, down the street, a house was being built. One day we took some bricks from the construction site to our house in

---

1   Jeremiah 17:9

our wagon. They were not many. For the contractor, a few bricks were of no importance. But when Dad came home from work and saw the bricks, he saw, not their insignificant value in the monetary sense, but their very significant moral value.

"Arthur, Harold, Paul: Where did you get these bricks?"

"We found them lying around."

"Lying around! They were taken from the place where they are making that house, right?"

We could no longer look Dad in the face, but instead had our eyes fixed on the floor when we answered yes. He ordered us to take the bricks back to the place where we had taken them. We thought Dad would forget, but the next day when he came home from work, he called me:

"Harold, did you take the bricks?"

"N...no, I...I forgot" (nice excuse).

It went on like that for a few days, until we were convinced that Dad would neither forget the matter nor let us escape. So it was that one day, three boys with heads hanging went with their wagon loaded with bricks to unload it behind the pile, trying to arrive from behind so that the workers would not see them. We will never forget that lesson as long as we live.

How many parents would be satisfied with the first evasive answer: *We found them lying around!*

We must attack the lies in us. Did we ever deceive them?

"Shut up, boy, or the cat will come and eat you."

"Don't do that, or an ugly witch will come and take you away."

So many such lies are used to frighten children and, by deception, to gain their obedience. Sooner or later the child learns that cats do not eat children and that the ugly witch is a hoax. So the parents pass for liars, and they are.

3. **PUNISHMENT SHOULD BE MEASURED ON THE BASIS OF THE MORAL VALUE OF THE OFFENSE.**
   I have seen parents severely punish a child for dropping a plate and breaking it, and laugh instead at hearing obscene words uttered by the child's tongue. Dropping a plate is an accident that involves no fault other than carelessness, and therefore deserves no more than a warning or an instruction on the necessary care. But indecent words compromise moral values and deserve strong punishment.

4. **CHILDREN SHOULD BE PUNISHED DECISIVELY.**
   Scolding and lightly spanking every now and then is a way of punishing of little or no value; that is *provoking your children to anger.* If the offense deserves punishment, one should be applied so that the child remembers and does not repeat the offense.

5. **THE ONE WHO PUNISHES MUST NOT BE ANGRY.**
   We heard of an irritated mother who hit a child on the head with a thick firewood log, for a petty offense. This

is unfair and dangerous. A child could even die this way. Blows to the head or back, especially in the lumbar region, over the kidneys, or in the abdomen, are dangerous and easily cause serious and permanent damage.

Apart from the danger of physical harm to the child, there are psychological and moral dangers. First, the child understands whether his parent is punishing him because he is upset, or whether it is for just reasons. In the first case, the punishment provokes the child's anger. Moreover, when parents are angry, there is a danger of punishing unjustly and much more severely than the offense deserves. Therefore, if you are angry, wait until your anger passes; then call the child, explain the reasons and notify him/her what his/her punishment will be.

6. **A VARIETY OF PUNISHMENTS MUST BE INVENTED.**
   Some children are of such a nature that the more discipline they receive, the harder they become. But, on the other hand, they are very sensitive. If they are denied a candy, or a walk, or a playtime, it gets under their skin.

It only takes a little imagination to invent a punishment well suited to the case, which produces the desired result: repentance and correction.

7. **ANY INJUSTICE COMMITTED AGAINST CHILDREN MUST BE CORRECTED.**
   "To err is human, to forgive, divine," says a popular proverb. Because we are human, we are prone to err and to punish our children unjustly. If we discover that we have punished a child unjustly, we should immediately

go to the child and confess our mistake and correct it. It is fair. We should not believe that, because we are older, we have the right to violate children's sense of justice. On the contrary, since their feelings are delicate and they are in their formative period, we must be more careful not to wound them.

An injustice against a child remains as a thorn, hurting their delicate feelings. Many carry such thorns in their souls until death. Because of this violence, parents lose their children's trust, respect and finally their love. Once lost, it is almost impossible to recover them.

Two of our children were fighting over a toy. I ordered the older to give it to the younger to end the quarrel and to teach the older to give preference to the younger. Later I found the older child in a room, crying inconsolably. I asked him why he was crying. He replied:

"But, Dad, that toy was mine. I bought it with my own pennies that I had saved, and it was mine."

I understood the injustice of what I had done and the depth of the wound in his heart. I apologized and ordered the other to return the toy to its rightful owner. Both were pleased.

8. PROMISES MUST BE SCRUPULOUSLY KEPT.
"Well, Johnny, stay here at home with your little sister and Isidra, and when we come back, we'll bring you some candy."

With these words Johnny's father and mother said goodbye to go to the neighboring city and return after a few hours.

When Johnny heard the car turning the corner on the way back, he ran to the door shouting:

"My candies, my candies!"

The mother saw him and heard his voice. She said to her husband:

"Oh! We forgot the candy. Do not stop the car. Go around the block to a bodega, to buy candy."

It was impossible not to keep our word to Johnny; for him the candies represented his parents' word of honor. Johnny was three years old at the time. He is now a man. He retains absolute trust in and deep respect for his parents. Why? Because the candies and so many other similar things were fulfilled.

Finally, as a roof ridge, let us add that the Scriptures command to correct the child. Some psychologists of our time teach that children should not be forbidden to do anything, so that inhibitions are not formed in their minds. The child should be allowed to express and develop his or her personality without inhibitions, so that complexes do not form in the mind, personality or emotions.

All this goes against the Bible, which is the best manual of psychology ever written or yet to be written. The child needs correction, he or she needs direction and instruction, and above all, he or she needs to feel security and confidence in something greater than himself or herself. This confidence is inspired by parents who exercise loving discipline. Parents who keep their word, who establish sound rules in the home and demand compliance with them, give that stable, secure, trustworthy something that is the primary need in the child's mind. This is the full result of true love between parents and children.

"Children, obey your parents in everything, for this pleases the Lord."[2] *"Foolishness is bound up in the heart of a child; The rod of correction will drive it far from him."* [3] *"He who withholds punishment hates his son, but he who loves him corrects him at an early age."* [4]

If we apply "the rod of correction" according to these rules, we will do so in a way that will not provoke our children to anger and they will not become discouraged. Thus, with the guidance and work of God's Holy Spirit in our homes, we will raise wise children who will bring joy to their fathers and not foolish children to the sorrow of their mothers.

"For the Lord disciplines the one he loves, just as a father, the son he delights in." (Proverbs 3:12 HCSB)

---

2   Colossians 3:20 HCSB
3   Proverbs 22:15
4   Proverbs 13:24 MT

CHAPTER V

The Windows

TEMPERANCE IN THE POSITIVE ASPECT OF CHILD DISCIPLINE

If the first part of this verse alludes to negative discipline and its abuses, this part speaks of the positive aspect of it. It speaks to us about raising our children, directing their development with intelligence and guiding their activities. It speaks of disciplining them in the sense of teaching and instructing them. And it tells us that all this must be done in the Lord, that is, under divine guidance, with everything correctly related to God and to his Son Jesus Christ. It imposes upon us the obligation to guide them in the wisdom whose principle is the fear of Jehovah.

If negative discipline places prohibitions and correction as a roof over the family's head, positive discipline enables them to enjoy temporal and eternal life, and gives them a correct perspective on the realities of life. Its precepts are like windows that open to allow a view of the beauties of the earth that God has prepared.

Positive and instructive discipline requires study and preparation. Parents need to carefully observe the character and development of each child. Children are individuals; they are different from each other. Therefore, each must be considered and managed individually.

If a child gets sick, parents run to the doctor. But many view with indifference the moral illnesses and disorders of their children's mental and intellectual development.

A father had neglected the moral and religious upbringing and instruction of his son. When he grew up, the son was a criminal and spent a long time running from the Law. The father, now an old man, lived alone. Late one night, the son showed up at the house and invited him out to the woods to see something. He led him to an old tree, twisted and ugly. He ordered his father to straighten out the tree and threatened to kill him if he didn't straighten it out right away.

The father, taken aback, answered:

"Son, how can you possibly demand such a thing of me? If the tree were new and the wood tender, I would apply some rods to the trunk to make it grow straight; but the wood is hard now and is impossible to straighten out."

"I am that tree," replied the son. "When I was a boy, you should have straightened me out; but now I'm old and hard, and it's impossible to straighten me out."

Let us study, then, and make great efforts so that our children grow up straight. As an aid to this arduous task, I propose another set of rules:

46

1. THE RELIGIOUS LIFE OF THE HOME MUST BE GIVEN PRIMARY IMPORTANCE.

Parents are to live Christian lives consistent with their religious profession. A father cannot teach his children to be meek and humble if he himself has his outbursts of anger. He cannot teach his children purity of thought and conversation if in moments of carelessness or anger he blurts out unseemly words. A mother cannot teach her daughter to be truthful if she sends her to answer the door: *Mom is not at home.*

We know Christian parents whose children do not follow the way of the Lord. We have asked ourselves, why? We have observed that there is almost always some serious inconsistency in the life of the parents. It is that the father and mother fight and do not agree, or that the father rules the house with shouting and despotism, or that the mother nags. Parents should live exemplary Christian lives, so that they can say: *"Be imitators of me, as I am of Christ."*

One winter morning, a father left his house for work. He had the habit of going into the bar on the corner to have his morning drink. During the night a light snow had fallen, leaving clear marks of his footprints. Suddenly he heard a voice:

"Daddy, look, Daddy."

It was his little son who had gone out after him. The child came stretching his little steps to plant his feet in his father's footsteps.

"Look, daddy, how I can put my feet in the same footprints as yours."

The father was thoughtful, very thoughtful. His son followed his footsteps to the bar. From that day on he never entered the bar again.

We have already spoken about family prayer, but here we mention it in its relation to children. Family worship should be done within the reach of the youngest child in the home. Sing a children's hymn or chorus. Read a short and easy portion that children can understand. Explain the story or portion read in simple words. Keep the prayer short and simple. Teach each child to pray in words he or she understands. The prayers of children are precious music in the ears of God.

And, finally, let parents pray and work until every child is truly reborn. Do not be fooled. Take nothing for granted. Don't think that your children are little angels from heaven. Soon you will smell smoke on their wings! Do not believe that a child is born again because he sings hymns and says his memory verse in Sunday school.

Job rose early to make sacrifices and pray for his children, for he said, "Perhaps my children have sinned, and blasphemed God in their hearts." Do the same. Pray for them and do not be satisfied until you are sure that they are all true Christians.

2. THE FAMILY'S ACTIVITIES MUST BE MONITORED AND DIRECTED.
We have talked about the need for the family to do things together: eating together at the table, reading together, playing together, working together. In relation to positive discipline, there is something more to say.

Parents should make a special effort and study about the conversation around the table. This can become very interesting and instructive, or it can degenerate into inane chatter of no value. Some learn Bible verses or portions of the Bible by heart during one of the meals of the day. They repeat the verses already learned and then learn a new one. Others use riddles in which one chooses the name of a biblical or historical character and the others try to figure out which one it is, by means of questions that can be answered with a yes or a no.

Word games and word studies are interesting and profitable, with paronymous words, for example.

"How do you spell 'there,' as in 'that place'?"

"T-h-e-r-e."

"Right. And how do you spell 'their' as in 'their house'?"

"T-h-e-i-r."

"Excellent! And how do you spell the contraction of 'they are'?"

"T-h-e-y-'-r-e."

"Very good!"

So the conversation continues until someone looks up the words in the dictionary. Our language abounds in similar words and other very interesting things. Even preschoolers learn something from these conversations.

It is necessary to vary such things so that they do not become annoying. Sometimes a child will want to talk about the game of baseball or another sport. In everything it is up to the parents to carefully direct the conversation, making sure that it is of common interest, and that it does not touch on topics that are not proper.

In addition, parents should play with their children and work with them in order to cultivate their companionship.

3. CHILDREN SHOULD BE GIVEN SOMETHING CONSTRUCTIVE AND EDIFYING TO DO.
It is not enough to tell the child not to do this or that. They must be given something else to occupy them. Their minds are active, full of curiosity, and their bodies full of energy. If good things are not found to occupy them, the devil will give them something to do. He has jobs for idle hands.

We have seen three- or four-year-old girls with needle and thread, learning to sew. How proud they are of their work! On the island of Margarita I saw a little girl, no more than four years old, with a knapsack of eggs and milk bottles hanging from her head and a spindle in her hand, spinning. The child who nails four tin lids on a slat to make a cart enjoys his cart more than the pretty painted one his father buys him. It costs less and the child learns more.

Among the Christmas presents my four-year-old grandson received, there was a tool kit: a hammer, a hand drill, a screwdriver, a saw. This is the gift that pleased him the most and that he carries with him wherever he goes. When his father was ten years old, I made him a little carpentry bench and bought him some tools. Every birthday or Christmas we bought him another tool for his workshop. He and his siblings spent many hours making carts, tables and other things. They learned to love to work, to handle tools and, above all, they lost their attraction to the street.

We visited a home where the twelve-year-old son took us to his room. He proudly showed us his aquarium. He had fish, toads, turtles and other aquatic life that he was studying scientifically. Someday that young man will be a marine veterinarian. What would have been the outcome if his mother had told him:

"No, get them out of here! You can't have those toads in the house!"?

One boy likes toads, another likes hammers; one girl will want to sew and another to paint. The point is for parents to encourage and assist and direct their children in such activities. The boy with the toads will become a doctor; the boy with the hammer, an engineer; the girl who sews, a mother; and the girl who paints, an artist. But if their parents discourage them, send them to throw those toads away, they may become hobos.

4. **YOU HAVE TO GIVE THEM SOME RESPONSIBILITY AND SEE THAT THEY FULFILL IT.**

The three-year-old can learn to put his clothes away in the closet. The six-year-old can learn to clean her room. The twelve-year-old can be responsible for washing the dishes after dinner or preparing breakfast. The important thing is to assign each one some work, adjusted to his age and ability, that he has to do every day.

If a task is assigned and we do not demand its fulfillment, we have done nothing but teach them unreliability.

"Peter, please pick up the garbage."

An hour later the mother finds Peter playing ball and the garbage not picked up. She should not ask John, who is not playing, to pick up the garbage. She must order Peter to stop his game and do as he is told; then he can play. The lesson will have to be firmly repeated several times, but in the end Peter will learn that work comes first, then play. But if we let Peter run away sometimes, we lose the battle and Peter will never learn to be responsible.

Of course, we should not always assign unpleasant jobs, nor for the sake of partiality give all the unpleasant jobs to only one of the children. But every child must learn that the unpleasant task must be accomplished when it is his turn. It is a fact of life that we all have to do some things we don't like. It is good for the child to learn this lesson.

5. IT IS NECESSARY TO CULTIVATE COMPANIONSHIP AND TRUST.

I was sitting, repairing an ordinary watch on the table. Our oldest son, who was three years old, climbed up on a chair and pushed his little head under my arm.

"Daddy, I want to see how the watch is fixed."

What was I supposed to do? Say: "Get out of here! You're going to break something! Go on, go away, I'm busy!"?

Would it have been the right thing to talk to him like that? That way I would have pushed my son away and hurt his feelings, which are worth more than a watch. I put him in a chair where he could see without touching. He is now a man. He knows how to repair fine watches and do many other jobs. Best of all, he has always been very close to his father.

A girl says:

"Mommy, I want to help you do the dishes."

"No, child. What you're going to do is break dishes. Get out of my way, you're in my way."

The girl leaves in tears, with a wounded heart. The mother continues to grumble:

"That impertinent girl, she always wants to butt in where she doesn't belong."

The mom doesn't understand that she has missed a precious opportunity to cultivate her daughter's companionship and trust and to teach her something. When she reaches adolescence and needs the advice and confidence that only her mother can give her, the girl will go looking for evil companions to receive perverse instruction. And the mother will ask, why?

A young lady said of another young lady she knew well: There is nothing that enters her mind that she does not tell her mother.

Why does that young lady feel so much confidence in her mother? Because since she was a little girl, her mother cultivated her companionship. They worked together, read together, talked together, and never did her mother hurt their tender feelings.

6. **IT IS NECESSARY TO KNOW WHERE THE CHILDREN ARE AND WHAT THEY ARE DOING.**

    It is better to have the neighbors' children come and play with our children in our yard. It gives some discomfort to the mother, but she can know what they're doing and what they're talking about. When they run and fight and scream, they are fine. But when they are hidden and quiet, who knows what they are doing or talking about!

We were late for a special service. The temple was packed with people. My partner and I stood in the courtyard, listening through the window. Some of the attendees' sons and daughters were in the yard playing. We soon realized that something obscene was going on between them. The parents were in the temple, very unconcerned, with their eyes on the things of God, while in the courtyard the devil was taking away their children.

Fathers, mothers, you need to know where your children are and what they are doing. We must not close our eyes to reality. The world and the devil have thousands of ways to corrupt the minds of our children. "Bad conversations corrupt good morals."

7. **THE HOME MUST BE MADE ATTRACTIVE IN SUCH A WAY THAT THE CHILDREN WANT TO BE IN IT.**

The living room should be neat, attractive, and well lit. Here young children will play and sit with their parents to read booklets or listen to Bible stories being read. Here the older children will spend hours reading, singing, playing, studying or chatting with their friends after dinner. But if the room is not attractive, they will want to go out on the street, to the movies or to the bar. These places are well lit. Their owners know that light attracts.

Some will object that they cannot afford to make the home attractive due to poverty. Fancy furniture is not necessary. The cost of lighting is minimal. We must make a sacrifice and an effort to make our homes attractive to our children. This is as necessary as food and clothing. The cleanliness, the good light and the friendly spirit are the three attractions.

In the living room of my parents' home there was a piano, bought with sacrifice, because they were poor. All the children received music lessons, another expense made with sacrifice. One brother played the trumpet. We spent many happy hours playing. Our classmates would come to our house and we would study together. My sister would prepare something sweet to serve. Mom, now a widow, was always with us; a good companion, a counselor, but never a nag. Even non-evangelical friends enjoyed this friendly atmosphere and preferred it to the street. A Christian testimony was maintained in everything. Mom knew where her children were and what they were doing, because she made every effort to keep the home attractive to them and their friends.

This positive discipline requires sacrifice, work and temperance; but it produces in children a love of the good and the beautiful, and an appreciation and perspective of the realities of life.

CHAPTER VI

The Garden

CHILDREN ARE PEOPLE

Malachi prophesied: *"He will turn the hearts of the fathers to the children, and the hearts of the children to their fathers, lest I come and strike the earth with a curse."* (Malachi 4:6)

Thus ends the Old Testament. Apart from the prophetic significance of this portion, there is here implied a universal moral principle: When harmony and communication between parents and children are lost, and when this becomes a general condition in any country, a curse falls upon that nation.

This lack of love and understanding is mainly due to selfishness and the fact that children are not recognized as persons.

Alfred was eleven years old and his little brother was one and a half years old when Esther was born. A few days later Alfred asked:

"Mommy, will Johnny know that Esther is a little person?"

Yes, Johnny knew that. A few nights before the baby sister was born, the parents wanted Johnny to occupy a new bed so that the baby could occupy the crib. But Johnny did not want to give up his crib. The night Esther was born, Johnny lay in her crib. In the morning he woke up in his new bed and saw his baby sister in the crib. He never laid claim to his crib. Another person had arrived, and it was hers.

In many ways parents violate the personal dignity of their children. This alienates children from their parents. This disrupts communication and harmony.

The world was shocked by the news of an 18-year-old girl who was murdered along with her hippy lover. She had enjoyed all the comforts of life. But the news reveals two things:

1) Both parents were divorced and remarried, and she was born of this union. There were five siblings, children of the mother or father. 2) She said that "my parents made me cringe; they were always yelling at me." That negative parental attitude mattered more to her than all the comforts of wealth.

Some parents yell and treat their children in a way they would never do in their business relationships, or with a servant. Children are people and should be talked to like people.

A little six-year-old girl stood in the doorway and asked:

"And you, where are you going?"

She asked this question of the grandfather who was leaving the house.

Why this lack of respect? Her tone of voice and emphasis were exactly the same as her mother's, who had asked the girl the same question more than once.

"Where are you going, daughter? Did you ask mom for permission?"

This would have been a much more courteous way and would have respected the child's dignity.

When the United States entered the First World War, military units were installed in all high schools and universities so that young people could train while they studied. In one school, an English teacher who had had some military instruction years ago was given the task of organizing a detachment. He positioned his boys and gave them the order:

"To the right, *please.*"

He forgot to say *go.* The boys laughed along with him. This means that *please* is not an expression of command.

Of course, we must teach our children, by example, to be polite and to say *please* and *thank you very much.* But we must recognize that *please* is not an expression to command. And when used as such, it soon degenerates.

"Sir, please...," says a father to his son in a threatening tone, meaning, "Hey you, if you don't do it, I'll beat you with my belt."

In conversation, *excuse me* can mean *liar*. It's all in the tone of voice and the disposition of the heart. A bad tone of voice and a bad attitude from the heart break communication.

"Peter, why didn't you do what I told you to do?" And the mother's voice trails away until it ends in tears. But with this expression little Peter has been told that she gives up, that he is the one in charge and that he does not have to obey his mother. In such a case, little Peter has not been treated as a responsible person. He is begged, he is flattered as if he were a two-footed monster, and he will soon become a two-footed monster. And the distance between little Peter and his mother grows bigger.

Another mistake is to set a deadline for the child to start obeying; for example, counting to ten.

"One, two..., three, fo...ur, (hurry), fi...ve, six, se...ven, eight..., nine... (I'm going to say it now), te...e...en." Before hearing the e with the n Robert moves.

A friend noticed a father who sent his son to do something and started counting in rhythm:

"One, two..." and before he got to three the boy was obeying. A good idea: They have until the count of three.

So, I figure they can move on three as well as on ten.

This begs the question, why count? No businessman ever gives his employee ten or three counts to execute an order. An instruction given, in a dignified manner to an intelligent person, expects due compliance. Other methods are an invitation to disobedience or a test to measure patience, to see how long it may take to begin to obey, and increase the distance between parent and child. The Lord said: *"But let your 'Yes' be 'Yes,' and your 'No,' 'No.' For whatever is more than these is from the evil one." (Matthew 5:37)*

Embarrassing a child in front of people is one of the worst things you can do. If the child needs a reprimand or punishment, call him aside, or wait until the punishment can be administered privately and calmly. The child does not resent a just punishment when he understands the reason. But when the shame of having it administered in the presence of others is added to the punishment, it becomes unjust and produces resentment and moral wounds that alienate the child from his parents.

Well known is the mother who tells visitors about her son Jimmy's antics in his presence.

"For example, my Jimmy; he is such an active boy that he can't sit still; and there is nothing he can't invent to annoy me... Jimmy! What are you doing? ...Well, as I was saying...." Of course, Jimmy had to show his mischief right then and there: His mom had told him so.

Why does Jimmy's mother want to talk about his terrible behavior? Is it to gain the sympathy of her friends, or to justify her poor relationship with her son? The latter are selfish motives and are not born of true love.

And yelling at a child? It demonstrates a basic lack of self-control and parental love. The use of phrases of irony or sarcasm and the ungracious use of polite words, demonstrates a basic lack of love and understanding. Sometimes polite words are used to cover up ungracious thoughts, and overly loving expressions to cover up a basic lack of love.

There are parents who do not love their children: They are a nuisance to them. But they seek to hide the true condition of the heart. Don't kid yourself: Kids recognize that. They can distinguish between true love and hypocrisy. They are attracted to the former and move away from the latter.

A little girl said:

"I like my dad, but not my mom, because she yells at me and talks to me ugly."

At school this girl was asked to write a short story. Here is her effort: "Once upon a time there was a little girl and her mother died; and she was sent to an orphanage where she lived happily ever after."

Tragic! Yes. Ask the Lord to reveal to you if such a tragedy is unfolding in your home.

Children are people. Let us recognize their dignity as people and treat them like people.

CHAPTER VII

The Plants in the Garden

CHILDREN ARE TO BE HELD IN ESTEEM

The prophet puts in the first place the turning of the heart of the
parents to the children; the turning of the heart of the children
to the parents follows logically. The parents must love first; the
children will love because they were loved first. We can deduce
from this the following corollary: Alienation begins with
the parents.

To get to the heart of the matter, I will ask some very personal
questions.

You can answer them to the Lord in your heart. Mother, when
you found out you were pregnant, were you angry or resentful?
Father, did you get angry and blame the wife when she announced
the situation to you? These attitudes result in an unwanted and
rejected child. This is part of what St. Paul said when he gave as

a characteristic of the end times the presence of men *"without natural affection." (2 Timothy 3:3 KJV)*

"Behold, children are a heritage from the Lord; the fruit of the womb is a precious thing." (Psalm 127:3 MT)

Our modern age believes itself wiser than the inspired word of Psalm 127. But it is not. *"For my thoughts are not your thoughts, neither are your ways my ways, saith Jehovah. For as the heavens are higher than the earth, so are my ways higher than your ways, and my thoughts than your thoughts." (Isaiah 55:8–9 ASV)*

Although the unwanted child is also unloved, he or she is sometimes the object of great ostentation of affection. This is a defense mechanism to hide the true condition of the heart, and is hypocrisy. Parents give the child many things, but give nothing of themselves. They are profuse in sweet words while being able to make cutting remarks with words of affection. The child understands this hypocrisy and rebels.

Parents, this is sin. Confess it and turn away from it. Ask the Lord for true love for your children, and then begin to give them of yourselves. Let me write down an example.

On one of our furloughs from missionary work, already celebrating our silver wedding anniversary, my wife and I agreed to finish our university studies. We lived with our three youngest children in a mobile home and another attached room. The youngest was almost five years old. On one occasion, after dinner and in the midst of the rush of theses and exams, I spent about half an hour in a simple hand game with the little girl. I will never forget the joy with which she jumped up and down saying:

"My daddy played with me! My daddy played with me!"

I had given her a little bit of myself. It would have been worth it to do poorly on an exam, but I didn't do poorly.

The saying that "children should be seen, but not heard" is not true. What is true is that children should not be allowed to monopolize the conversation. But notice that the rejected boy is the one who misbehaves and tries to get all the attention from people. Better is attention with displeasure than no attention at all!

At the dinner table or in the living room, even when there are visitors, children should be included in the conversation. This should not be done as a concession, but in a natural way, accepting them as people.

One of the first lessons we had to learn as foreign missionaries was that it is a great lack of civility to speak English with our companions if a person who does not understand English is present. It is a very common and deeply felt fault, and rightly so. Would it be less polite to talk only about adult topics in the presence of children? The conversation should be made enjoyable for all ages present and everyone should participate in the conversation. Adult matters can be discussed with visitors after the children have left.

At Wheaton Evangelical College in Wheaton, Illinois, USA, graduating students are required to take the formidable comprehensive exams. One of these exams is for the major subject studied in the entire four-year course. The other is a humanities or general culture exam. A young lady graduating from the music conservatory not only did well in music, but she got the highest grades in humanities there had been in several years. The director of the conservatory called her to ask how she had achieved that. She replied:

"I've always loved to read, and at home we talk about everything at the dinner table and study together every night."

Mealtime at the home of one of the nicest families I have ever met was a special treat. And it wasn't so much because of the food, because sometimes they were broke. But there was always interesting and lively conversation, and there were riddles and word games; "mental gymnastics," the father of the family called them. All the children participated, all six of them. Was it worth it? Now they are all adults and some are approaching gray hair. They are alert, agile-minded people, and each is achieving success in their profession.

Another dignity that should be given to children, as persons, is to make them partners in family projects. It was nice to see a family working together, building their house. Teenagers worked alongside their father in the heaviest jobs. They learned how much a bucket of concrete weighs, and it didn't do them any harm. The children helped their mother paint and plant the grass and bushes. In a special way that house was their house. And none of those kids think their parents are too stern or tyrannical.

One of these young men, who is about to graduate from high school, was somewhat difficult to discipline as a child. His parents treated him with love, with firmness. Now he is closer to his parents than the others. At the same time, he has been so busy doing things with his father and learning from him that he hasn't had time to discover how much he himself knows and how backward and outdated the old man is.

There is a family that owns land in a national park. For many years they kept a herd and every year they took the cows to the park to supply milk to the tourists. With the earnings from this work, all of the children, in turn, went to college. They all worked happily on the family project of educating themselves. And they spent happy years and happy *vacations* in this way. Here is the record of that family: a university rector, a university professor, a doctor, two missionaries in Africa, an evangelical pastor's wife and an agricultural contractor who is an elder in his church.

As young people pass through adolescence to adulthood, they must be accorded the dignity and responsibility of their age. *"That our sons may be as plants grown up in their youth." (Psalm 144:12)*

There was a boarding school for missionaries' children that had from first grade to two years of college. Once the older youth were sent to the city for a conference and each was given one quarter to spend freely, as long as it was not on candy. One of the boys put his quarter into the offering. As he left the church he saw a quarter on the sidewalk, picked it up and bought candy. Then his conscience became pricked and he confessed it to the directors. Thank God there are boys of tender conscience; but this whole business is ridiculous. These people did not want to give their young people the dignity and responsibility of their age.

Another thirteen-year-old boy wrote to his parents, "Mrs. X called me into her office today to show me the banknote you sent me for my birthday, and for us to decide what flavor of ice cream we were going to buy with it for my birthday party." Who would make the decision? Mrs. X. Who was satisfied? Only she, because the boy knew that he was not the one who was going to make use of his birthday present.

Four years later that same boy was with his parents. His father gave him money to buy a hat. The boy was hesitant and said:

"Dad, let's both go pick out the hat."

"No, son, you buy the one you like best."

He immediately went out to buy a hat. He was old enough to make a decision.

Two fifteen-year-olds were given the somewhat delicate job of engraving some letters on wood. The owner instructed them in the art, down to the details of how to take the chisel in the hand and how to cut in relation to the grain of the wood, and showed them the places where there was danger of marring their work. After giving these proper instructions and watching them at work for a while, the owner went away, and left them on their own. The boys were surprised by this show of confidence and were encouraged to do a good job, and carved the letters out without a mistake. They were treated not as irresponsible little boys, but as responsible men, and they reciprocated.

Young people should not only be accorded the dignity and responsibility of their age, but should also be taught to make responsible decisions.

They cannot be thrown into the water with a "sink or swim." They must be shown the factors that go into a given situation so that they can make a responsible decision. Then they are made to understand that they are left with the decision and also the consequences, whether good or bad.

We learn things by making mistakes, by trial and error. Of course, there are some mistakes with such severe consequences that they must be avoided at all costs. But we have to let our young people make some mistakes of their own, and by them learn. They should be admonished so that they do not make the same mistake twice. We of the passing generation made more mistakes than necessary, and we still do.

The whole point of this matter is that we treat youth as responsible people. This treatment will suppress rebellion and win the admiration and affection of young people. All of these things, along with consistent Christian teaching and example in the home, will be used by the Lord to *turn the hearts of the children toward the parents.*

CHAPTER VIII

The Years of Ripe Fruit

THE REWARDS OF TEMPERANCE

The popular opinion is that the years of old age are fruitless, bitter and full of sorrows. There is no shortage of examples that can be cited in confirmation of this opinion. But it doesn't have to be that way.

Husbands and wives who in their youth formed a Christian home and brought up their children in the discipline and admonition of the Lord, have laid a good foundation and sown good seed for the years of a mature age that will be happy and rich in its most delicate fruits. Let's see what the Scriptures say:

"The mercy of the LORD is from everlasting to everlasting on those who fear him, and his righteousness to children's children." (Psalm 103:17)

"Yes, may you see your children's children. Peace be upon Israel! (Psalm 128:6)

75

"The silver-haired head is a crown of glory, if it is found in the way of righteousness." (Proverbs 16:31)

"Children's children are the crown of old men, and the glory of children is their father." (Proverbs 17:6)

These promises of God are for the righteous, justified by faith and walking on the path of Christ's righteousness. These promises rest on God's faithfulness. Even in times of adversity and national judgment, the prophet Jeremiah cried out: *"Through the Lord's mercies we are not consumed, because His compassions fail not. They are new every morning; great is your faithfulness." (Lamentations 3:22–23)*

It is through the maturity of years of experience that we come to delve into these words of the Lord. What are these delicious fruits of the ripe years?

The passage of time imparts to Christian parents a deep trust in God's faithfulness. They have been through many trials and have seen how God makes all things work together for good for those who love Him. They have seen how, though the righteous falls seven times, he rises again. *(Proverbs 24:16)* Fleeting tests are no longer intimidating. The years of toil and trouble have passed and, although there are still trials ahead, the soul is filled with a serenity that sings: *"GREAT IS YOUR FAITHFULNESS"*.

The companion of this confidence is the peace of God that surpasses all understanding. *"Do not be anxious about anything, but in every situation, by prayer and petition, with thanksgiving, present your requests to God. And the peace of God, which transcends all understanding, will guard your hearts and your minds in Christ Jesus." (Philippians 4:6–7 NIV) "Great peace have those who love Your law, and nothing causes them to stumble." (Psalm 119:165)*

From this trust and peace is born a perspective of the eternal. Or is it that from this perspective acquired over time comes confidence in the faithfulness of the eternal God, and hence peace? So closely related are these things that it is difficult to discover which is cause and which is effect. St. John wrote: *"I have written to you, fathers, because you have known him who is from the beginning." (1 John 2:14)*

Parents remember the time when their children did not exist, a time of which the children can never have a memory, a time that for them belongs to the eternal past. Thus, in a small degree, the parents have knowledge of Him who is from the beginning.

Moreover, with the passage of time they have seen fashions, opinions, rulers, and scientific and philosophical theories change; they have come to understand that all these things are like the tossing of the seas, and that *"The Eternal God is your refuge, and underneath are the everlasting arms." (Deuteronomy 33:27)*

From this perspective, temporary things lose their value and charm. The disappointments of life no longer hurt the parents, because they see the eternal, the things that do not change, the One who is the same today, yesterday and forever.

"And you shall see your children's children." What a deep satisfaction it is to see one's children now men and women who take on the

responsibilities of life and achieve the successes we so desired for them! *"A wise son makes a father glad."* [1] How great is this joy!

Then the grandchildren. Grandparents no longer care for them, because God has entrusted them to younger and stronger hands. They enjoy them without the pains of their upbringing. They enjoy hearing their first words, and when they begin to learn their first letters. They receive a deep and ineffable joy in hearing their little prayers, their songs to God and their first manifestations of faith in the Savior. This ripe fruit is so sweet that just thinking about it brings tears of joy.

In addition to the carnal lineage there is the spiritual lineage, if we have been faithful witnesses of the grace of our Savior. It was said of the Lord: *"He shall see his offspring, he shall prolong his days; the will of the Lord shall prosper in his hand. He shall see the fruit of the travail of his soul and be satisfied...".* [2] The Lord had no fleshly offspring, but by His death and resurrection He became the progenitor of a spiritual lineage that is eternal. We cannot be redeemers; but it is given to us, in a certain sense, to enter into this work and, through our testimony, to beget spiritual children.

What a satisfaction it is to see the fruit of our testimony! Then others are seen who have believed through them, and so the spiritual generation continues and grows.

There are Christian couples who offer friendship, confidence and understanding to young people in their homes. Some of these young people are converted and go out to other places, carrying

---

1   Proverbs 15:20
2   Isaiah 53:10–11 RSV

the testimony and love of Christ. We know of a married couple now advanced in years who have not had children; but, in this way, they have a spiritual generation that has reached distant countries with the testimony of Christ. *"Even in old age they will bear fruit."*

Other fruits of the mature years are intercession, teaching and counseling. We read that when Samuel was old, the people of Israel asked for a king. Samuel felt the lack of gratitude of the people implied in this request. He understood that the people rejected him; but he did not let his spirit become embittered. *"Moreover, as for me, far be it from me that I should sin against the Lord in ceasing to pray for you; but I will teach you the good and the right way."* (1 Samuel 12:23)

Once retired from the cares and hardships of public life and the administration of the government of Israel, Samuel did not consider his work finished. He was engaged in intercession and teaching. In the opinion of some, the work he did in these years was greater than that of his public life. It is probable that in these years he founded the first of the schools of the prophets. These schools came to exert profound influence on the religious life of Israel.

Moral and spiritual teaching is work that lasts for eternity. Accompanied by intercession, the Spirit of God makes teaching produce lasting changes in the lives of students. *"I will teach you the good and the right way."* (NKJV)

The angel said to Daniel: *"Those who are wise shall shine like the brightness of the firmament; and THOSE WHO TURN*

*MANY TO RIGHTEOUSNESS, like the stars forever and ever".
(Daniel 12:3)*

*"Even in old age they will bear fruit." "And the work of righteousness
shall be peace, and the effect of righteousness, quietness and assurance
forever." (Isaiah 32:17) "All your children shall be taught by the
Lord, and great shall be the peace of your children." (Isaiah 54:13)*

Editor's Note: May the Lord grant that this book will serve you
as an inspiration for the fruitful education of your children; and
that, well armed with the weapons of Faith and Love, they may
attain happiness in this world and in the world to come.

Appendix A

Below is an excerpt from the poem *The Cotter's Saturday Night,*
by Robert Burns:

The cheerfu' supper done, wi' serious face,
They, round the ingle,[1] form a circle wide.
The sire turns o'er, with patriarchal grace,
The big ha'bible, ance[2] his father's pride:
His bonnet rev'rently is laid aside,
His lyart haffets[3] wearing thin and bare;
Those strains that once did sweet in Zion glide,
He wales[4] a portion with judicious care;
And "Let us worship God!" he says with solemn air.

They chant their artless notes in simple guise,
They tune their hearts, by far the noblest aim.
Perhaps Dundee's wild-warbling measures rise;
Or plaintive Martyrs, worthy of the name;
Or noble Elgin beets the heaven-ward flame;
The sweetest far of Scotia's holy lays:
Compar'd with these, Italian trills are tame;
The tickl'd ears no heart-felt raptures raise;
Nae unison hae[5] they with our Creator's praise.

---

1   ingle = fireplace
2   ha'bible = hall Bible; ance = once
3   lyart = gray; haffets = temples or sideburns
4   wales = sings [apparently]
5   nae = no; hae = have

The priest-like father reads the sacred page,
How Abram was the friend of God on high;
Or Moses bade eternal warfare wage
With Amalek's ungracious progeny;
Or how the royal bard did groaning lie
Beneath the stroke of Heaven's avenging ire;
Or Job's pathetic plaint, and wailing cry;
Or rapt Isaiah's wild, seraphic fire;
Or other holy seers that tune the sacred lyre.

Perhaps the Christian volume is the theme,
How guiltless blood for guilty man was shed;
How He, who bore in Heaven the second name,
Had not on earth whereon to lay His head:
How His first followers and servants sped;
The precepts sage they wrote to many a land:
How he, who lone in Patmos banished,
Saw in the sun a mighty angel stand,
And heard great Bab'lon's doom pronounc'd by
Heaven's command.

Then, kneeling down to Heaven's Eternal King,
The saint, the father, and the husband prays:
Hope "springs exulting on triumphant wing,"
That thus they all shall meet in future days,
There, ever bask in uncreated rays,
No more to sigh, or shed the bitter tear,
Together hymning their Creator's praise,
In such society, yet still more dear;
While circling Time moves round in an eternal sphere.

Compar'd with this, how poor Religion's pride,
In all the pomp of method, and of art;
When men display to congregations wide
Devotion's ev'ry grace, except the heart!
The Power, incens'd, the pageant will desert,
The pompous strain, the sacerdotal stole;
But haply,[6] in some cottage far apart,
May hear, well-pleas'd, the language of the soul;
And in His Book of Life the inmates poor enroll.

---

6   haply = by chance

Appendix B

The author originally used the Spanish Reina Valera Antigua and Reina Valera 1960 versions of the Bible. The translator made great efforts to find English verses that most resembled the Spanish verses in each context. As a result, a number of English versions were used. And when no English version could be found that resembled the Spanish closely enough, a special translation appearing only here was used, labelled MT (for text suggested by machine translation, which was often amazing).

Scripture quotations marked ASV are taken from the American Standard Version, in the public domain.

Scripture quotations marked DARBY are taken from The Darby Bible, in the public domain.

Scripture quotations marked EHV are taken from the Holy Bible, Evangelical Heritage Version® (EHV®) © 2019 Wartburg Project, Inc. All rights reserved. Used by permission.

Scripture quotations marked HCSB are taken from the Holman Christian Standard Bible®, Copyright © 1999, 2000, 2002, 2003, 2009 by Holman Bible Publishers. Used by permission. Holman Christian Standard Bible®, Holman CSB®, and HCSB® are federally registered trademarks of Holman Bible Publishers.

Scripture quotations marked KJ21 are taken from the 21st Century King James Version®, copyright © 1994. Used by permission of Deuel Enterprises, Inc., Gary, SD 57237. All rights reserved.

Scripture quotations marked KJV are taken from the King James Version, in the public domain.